DEDICATION

To Hannah and Hailey, my girls, my world. You are my moon, my sun and my stars. May you always find light on the journey.

Presentation by *BookLeaf Publishing*

Web: www.bookleafpub.com

E-mail: info@bookleafpub.com

ISBN: 9789358319699

First edition 2023

She Rises

Kristin Schaaf

India | USA | UK

Light

Letting go
Is like coming home
To an unfamiliar place
Where she feels unwelcome
And the dust doesn't settle
The clanging outside
Is deafening inside
Amplifying the noise
Muffling the truth
It keeps getting louder
So loud she can't stand it
Yet she turns up the volume
And can't stop listening
Because the silence is
Even louder
It exposes the fears
The words she carries
The loneliness she hides
The deep wounds inside
Needing validation
Illumination
Consecration
Less condemnation
Freedom from guilt
Reparation

Because all that keeps her
From giving into the
Darkness
Is believing
And walking into
The light.

Words

Falling
Is a lot easier
Than standing.
Awake
Is a lot harder
Than sleeping.

Speaking comes easy
But there is rarely a moment
Where she feels so eloquent
Perfecting her thoughts
Wanting her words to
Bring life
Inspire
Rather than swirl around
Dizzying themselves
In her mind
Words spoken
And unspoken
Words remembered
And forgotten.

Words change everything
Words thought
Words said

They blame
They inform
They uplift
Or they cut down
Words can transform
They can speak and
Tell a powerful story.

Her story is broken
Partially spoken
Mostly hidden
In the dark corners of her mind
Buried deep inside
She longs to find the words
To bring light
Give hope
Bring herself back.

Words can change
Words can free
She's no longer afraid
Letting go
Releasing the grip
The false security
Letting truth reign.

She doesn't have to fall
She can let herself be
Pick up the pieces

Shattered and glued.
No longer broken
Beaten or bruised
But mended
Renewed.

Words can heal
Transform a soul
Let the lost
Find themselves
Restored once again.

Her Shell

She falls, she feels
She knows what's real
It pierces her veins
It beats in her heart
She knows it well
It is her start
Of every day
From deep inside
The knowing herself
And who she is
The cocoon she's in
Has become her shell
She embraces the warmth
And wants to hide
From the voices who
Speak so many lies
Her chrysalis forms
She lets it shine
Even when shaken
Now is her time
To shed the layers
To form her wings
She lets herself
Begin to sing
The song of hope

She forgets the words
They're spoken back
She wraps them in light
Until they open
The darkest night
She spreads her wings
She sings her song
Now she knows
It won't be long
The shell breaks down
It hits the floor
Now she's ready
To fly out the door
She's bared it all
She's opened her heart
And now she has
A brand new start.

Warmth

Shadows dance
On the wall
As light pours in
She wants to fall
Instead she sees
The golden haze
She lifts her eyes
And starts to gaze
At what she knows
Brings so much life
And not within
The darkest night
She's let truth in
And poured lies out
She knows what this
Is all about
To love yourself
And letting go
Of what she's felt
Or thought she's known
The beauty lies
In trusting what's safe
Her body rests
In warmth and grace.

Rise and Fall

She rises, she falls
She tries to find her way
Hearing the quiet call
She doesn't want to stay
In this back and forth
Ping pong balls in her mind
The game is a battle
Against what she knows inside
The truth is buried
Deep inside her heart
She's ignored that voice
And doesn't know how to start
To trust in who she is
And what she really knows
Who she is made to be
She longs to truly grow
She sheds the thick skin
One layer at a time
She whispers to herself
I believe, I can try
To know she can go
Where she's made to be
Just trust in the voice
And then she will see
The beauty that she's made for

The rising of the sun
She's blossomed and she knows
Her life has just begun.

Sometimes

Sometimes falling
Feels like failing
Feels like breathing
Feels like believing
Feels like hoping
Feels like enduring.

Sometimes falling
Lifts us up
Gives us hope
Rises within us
From a place we
Never knew before.

The depths within
Breathe new life
Give us hope
Strength to endure
Light in the darkness.

Sometimes life
Gives us heartache
Knocks us over
Knees in the dirt
Face on the ground

Gasping for breath
Grasping for life
Not seeing the light
Hope buried in the depths.

Sometimes we rise
Rubbing the dirt
From our eyes
Squinting in the brightness
Shining its beam in the darkness
A lone star
Lighting the way
Guiding us north
Daring us to surrender
To love
To hope
To believe
The best is yet to come.

His Eyes, His Heart

His eyes smiled as he stared at her
Pools chocolate brown rimmed with gold
Tiny flecks of green in the light
Showing glimpses of his secrets
What he held beneath the surface
Rarely seen, those moments
In between
Laughter, love and quiet strength
His heart a mystery
Open yet sustaining so many stories
She loved the moments of vulnerability
His heart drew her in with
Intrigue, bold yet unassuming
Daring and brave
Holding more than she ever knew
Those eyes showed much more
Pain and fear held below
Yet he held on
Through his faith by grace
Until he was gone
When those eyes closed
She saw who was there
A man who fought to be strong
A man who loved more fully
Than she ever knew

Who brought more hope
Than she thought she had
She wanted to stay in that room forever
Bathed in his pools of chocolate
She couldn't look into but could still see
Her daughters now carrying
His vision, his heart
Everything he was made to be.

His Strength

She sees his calm assurance
Weathering the beating winds
His strength a mighty house
Built along a rushing river.

He always knew what he had
A flashing smile dripping with wit
He held her gaze for so long
She knew that he wouldn't quit
He'd never give up
Until she was his
And would never leave her side
He knew he'd do things just right
Until she became his bride.

That day came and he held on
Through every twist and turn
She felt his comfort and his grace
And he was always quick to learn
There was no task too small
Or too hard for him to try
He knew he had what it takes
With his family by his side.
That confidence she felt with him
Is what kept their family strong

Along with faith and friendships
They had nurtured for so long.

He brought so much peace
To the noise inside her mind
She didn't have to face her fears
All she had buried deep inside.

In times of stress and hardship
The voice would try to speak
The more she tried to silence it
The more she would feel weak.
"I believe in you" he told her
When she felt weighed by the lies
She knew with his support
She'd strengthen what was inside.

The story didn't end
When he was no longer there
She felt nervous and alone
As though no one really cared
But deep within she knew
She wasn't truly alone
So she found support she needed
And the strength to carry on.

His Ending, Her Beginning

She knows it won't be long now
The wait has been so long
The ache in her heart tells her
She will be singing her final song
She goes back for the encore
She sees what's no longer there
She's waited by the door
Waiting for his stare
His eyes no longer looking
His voice no longer speaks
She feels the waves come
Coursing down her cheeks
She lays her cheek to chest
Waiting for the rise and fall
She knows it's not coming
She has to accept it all
The weight is now hers to carry
Once she walks outside that door
She cannot fathom that story
She wanted so much more
Time was what she longed for
Memories to fill her heart
She'd no longer make new ones
She didn't know where to start
She stayed in that room for hours

Saying her final goodbyes
Memorizing the details of this moment
Wishing she could see his eyes
Staring deep within hers
Chocolate brown for days
Instead she smells his soapy skin
From where he somberly lays
She talks to him one more time
And then begins to pray
She will have the strength to go on
New mercies each and every day.

Breathe

Inhale, exhale
The breath calms her
Letting herself feel
Each rise and fall
Concentrating on the breath.

She feels more deeply
Than she's ever felt before
The fear is real
The pain goes deep
Yet she doesn't give in
She lets herself breathe
Breathe in life
Breathe out fear.

The unknown taunts her
Whispers in the dark
Shadows lurking around
The bend
It covets her mind
To give in to the worry
To stop trusting
Hoping
Believing.

Cancer is a sickness
But it cannot drive us
Away from the light
Into the darkness
Into fear.

We must hold tight
To the hope we profess
Cling to truth
Faith
The love that guides.

Don't be afraid
Dear one
Don't let yourself
Fall
Rise up
On eagle's wings
Where you will not
Grow weary.

Rest in my shadows
Lay your head
On my shoulders
Find rest
Peace
Home.

Her Healing

The depths called out to her
Pulling her in, singing their song
She couldn't ignore the whisper
So she went for what she longed
A deep knowing and a feeling
She had to completely give in
She couldn't quite recognize
What to do or how to win
The clattering and banging
Still ruminating in her mind
She thought the depths would quiet
The fears and worries inside
She then cried out for mercy
She finally couldn't let go
She knew she had to stop
It was time, she couldn't say no.

So then the door was open
She stepped timidly inside
She opened her world, her heart
To quiet the noise inside her mind
Every week she went back
For more than she knew she had
But for herself and her girls
She knew she would make it last.

The weeks went on
More time went by
Memories brought to her very core
She knew she'd need to face it all
To let herself finally cry
Be broken down to pieces
And try to understand
What it was that made her break
And what would help her stand.

The time had come to heal
She was ready to take it on
She had forgotten how to dance
And sing the very song
The strong spirit that she had
The day that she was born
And now she knew she had it
It was there all along
She embraced and carried with her
The nurturing voice within
It lovingly spoke with kindness
And she knew she could begin
Her life was far from over
She was finally going to start
Listening and trusting the voice
Whispers of God inside her heart.

Be Strong

Be strong
Be courageous
Paint on your brave face
Breathe in peace
Breathe out anxiety
Let the voice of truth
Drown out the doubt
Find your strength
From deep within
You are stronger
Than you think,
You say she's
Stronger
Than the weight
Of the anchor
That presses
So firmly
Its grip so heavy.

This strength she carries
Isn't a strength
She possesses
Within herself
It isn't something
She strives for.

She doesn't want to be brave
She doesn't have it in her
To be strong
She feels it, knows it in her bones
Strength, she realizes
Doesn't come from herself
Being strong doesn't mean
Casting aside fear
Or putting a bandage on her pain.

Strength, she realizes
Comes from surrender
To the unknown
To the truth
Getting up
Taking one step at a time
Letting herself be
Just as she is
Accepting herself
All of her feelings
All of her scars
She embraces the truth
That she is worthy
She is covered
She is strong
She is brave
Not because of anything she does
But because of who she is:

She shows up
Looks to the sun
Lets it radiate her beauty
Bathe her with glory
Magnify her light.

New Beginnings

She steps
Into the chasm
Into the unknown
Into tomorrow
Looking ahead
She follows the voice
That calls her
The door that is open
Is the only one she knows
The only one she trusts.

As this day ends and
The heavens twinkle
Crisp lights in the darkness
Illuminating the way
In the clear, dark night
The new day promises
New hope
New beginnings
New mercies
And she goes
One step at a time
There is something
She must choose
She must hold onto

And she knows
It is the only
Certainty she can cling to.

A love that promises
A love that perseveres
A love that never fails
A love that conquers all
A love that endures forever.

She Bends

She bends
Beneath the invisible anchor
Pressing its curves
Into the weight of her back
She gives in
To the heaviness
Pressing on
Not letting it break her
It slows her steps
Each one harder than the last
She moves forward
Looking ahead
Not behind her
Or too far into the distance.

She finds herself
Seeking safety, comfort
Finding herself surrounded
Clothed in a cocoon
Arms lifting her
Helping her carry the anchor
Its heaviness no longer
Overtaking, overbearing
So she can keep moving
Not alone, yet still seeking

Solace in the chaos.

She hides within the cocoon
Letting herself grow
Become shaped by the anchor
Giving into its weight
Knowing it is in the depths
She truly finds light
Discovers herself
Knows her beauty
And becomes something exquisite.

Worthy

It feels all too easy
To succumb to the pain
To give in to the voices
The lies that speak
Louder than she can stand
The whispers of truth
Fade into silence
The lies become louder
Enveloping her mind
Convincing with their false truths
Pushing to the forefront
Claiming her thoughts
Longing to be the victor
She shakes and stumbles
Falling to the ground
Her knees feeling weak
Yet heavy and weighted
The tears start to fall
Her heart cries
Deep cries out to deep
Longing for truth
To linger in her heart
To fill the depths
Overflow her being
Her mind no longer

Given over to the darkness
But filled with the light
Basking in its glow
Resting in its truth
Believing and knowing
She is enough
She is loved
She is free
She is redeemed
She is pursued
She is captivated
By the one
Who declares her
His beauty
His love
His daughter
Worthy of grace
Worthy of love
Worthy of healing
Worthy
Just as she is.

Snow

Darkness crashes
Into white
Casting shadows
Into the night
Illuminating beauty
Radiating light.

She stands in awe
Taking it all in
Letting the purity
Wash away what's within
Knowing the hope
That lets her begin
Again
And again
No longer bound
She is set free
To believe in love
Because of the victory.

Twinkling lights
Amidst the black
Tiny rays poking through
Giving strength where she lacks
The light is a veil

In the vastness of the sky
Providing a well
Where her soul runs dry.

Her lungs breathe in
The crisp night air
Cleansing and waiting
Knowing what's there
Beyond the veil
The victory's won
She knows tomorrow brings
The rising of the sun.

Tomorrow

Across the distance
She sees him
His soul gives way
Opening a chasm
Across a world between them
She doesn't want to stay
It feels too hard to open
To someone who won't know
Who can't give her what she needs
Someone she wants to let go.

His voice breaks through the silence
The brokenness in her heart
He opens something deep inside
His prayers a brand new start
He shows her endless beauty
When she can't see his face
He gives her so much love and light
And endless amounts of grace.

Never did she think
She would love across the miles
But here she knows deep within
The one who has given her smiles
He laughs and gives her so much hope

More than she could ever know
Is such an incredible gift
And she can't wait to see it grow.

Love Again

When the darkness fades
She opens her eyes
Lifts up her head
And sees the surprise
A soul she feels
She's known so long
One who knows
Her broken song
She quiets the voice
That tells her no
Though all that's within her
Doesn't want to go
She raises her hand
Opens her heart
She sees within him
A brand new start.

She feels his depths
And knows his gaze
He whispers to her
And quietly prays
His spirit speaks
His heart reaches her core
She hasn't heard
This song before

Its notes so beautiful
An enchanting melody
Pulling strings of her heart
The harp sets her free
To love again
To know what's real
She gives into God's mercy
To let herself feel
A love that is pure
One that's deep and so right
She sings praises to God
For his goodness and light.

Stained Glass

Cracked and broken
Her stained glass pieces
Glimpses of color
Covered with mist
Now shattered
Yet still beautiful
Radiating light
She cannot see
The rainbow shining
Its prism through
Her very core
She knows she has it
The strength to carry
The will to move
To know she's worthy
She takes her pieces
Bathes them in light
No longer bound
To the endless night
She looks ahead
To the shining sun
She sees the glory
Her life has just begun.

Be Still

Be still
And rest
Take refuge
Be blessed
By the one
Who can cover you
With the hope
That brings peace
Beyond understanding
Or circumstance
Breaking through
The deep sorrow
The piercing sadness
To bring rays of light
Shining in the darkness
Illuminating life anew
Beyond the shadows
That linger
Like a dark cloud passing by
The truth remains
That this is temporary
There is far greater
Beyond comprehension.

Yet the soul aches

Yearns, cries out
For healing
For strength
For freedom
Be free
Dear one
Let yourself fall
Float in the river
Of surrender
For it is letting go
Trusting in tomorrow
Finding faith in promises
And the Holy presence
That we find
The weight we carry
Isn't our burden or pain
What we hold onto
When we let ourselves
Be held
Is the weight
The freedom
Of glory.

Hope Rises

Hope rises
Steaks of burnt red and gold
Bursting forth its fire
From the black of night
Shedding its light
Into the depths
Closing in on the darkness
From where it came
Bringing with it a sense of purpose
Truth
Faith
Awareness
That beyond the darkness
There is no fear
Only belief
Only letting go
Only hope.

Listening to the voice
That calls her out
Of the shadows
Illuminating
Bringing life
Light
Fire

A glow
From within
That can only be found
From surrender
To the very thing
The very one
That calls her
Into the chasm
The great unknown
The place of trust
Where she truly
Believes and finds
A love that changes her
Refining her from within
A love that never fails
Now and forever.